Do We Really Reap What We Sow?

Application of the Laws of Harvest

Jonas Nguh, PhD.

GWW
PUBLISHING CO.

Do We Really Reap What We Sow ?

Copyright © 20187 by Jonas Nguh, PhD.

ISBN: 978-1-948829-14-4

First Edition: September 2018

Edited by:
LPW Editing & Consulting Services, LLC
www.litaward.org

Published by
Greater Working Women Publishing Company, LLC
www.gwwpublishing.com

10 9 8 7 6 5 4 3 2 1

CONTENTS

Preface

I can still remember my grandmother warning me about my choices in life. In her attempt to see that her grandson would behave himself, she used to say, "Don't forget, Jonas, you always reap what you sow ... Always!" And of course, she was right. But when most of us think of the concept of reaping what we sow, I have found we usually think of this in the negative sense. We think of paying the consequences for foolish choices, but the laws of the harvest are not just negative. These laws are also positive, very positive, and stand as a promise for sowing that which is good as well as a warning against sowing what is bad. I had the privilege of reading John Lawrence's book, Life's Choices. I found John's book to be tremendously rewarding and insightful. As an educator, I have applied these principles in my own life and seen it motivate and encourage many of my students in their academic and professional journeys, not so much because of the negative connotations—but because of the positive. The seven laws listed below come from John's excellent book and this narrative is a summary of those principles.

1

We Reap Only What Has Been Sown

L ife is filled with choices; choices that affect us on an everyday basis in everything we do. Importantly, this observation means our everyday choices are not without significance. Our choices affect others and us in dramatic ways whether we see it immediately or not. This narrative is not meant to intimidate us from making choices, for even a failure to make choices is still a choice.

Rather, it is designed to motivate us to wise choices, which we may redeem the benefits from. Do we realize the far-reaching implications of our choices on the lives of others—children, family members, co-workers, and friends? Being a good role model is a form of sowing that can result in reaping changes in the lives of others.

Life has a great deal to say about sowing and reaping. First, we must sow to reap. All walks of life have sowing and reaping. Lawyers, doctors, scientists, and professors spend long years in study. You reap excellence if you sow effort, but you have to sow to reap. I heard a story about a man who told his son, "Don't go into that watermelon patch. The melons aren't ripe yet." Then the father drove into town. The boy went out to the watermelon patch and found one melon that he knew was ripe. He pulled it, broke it over some rocks and ate it. After the act, he knew he had done wrong. He knew he had disobeyed his father, but he hadn't been caught. Several weeks passed. As the father was driving a cow up from the pasture, he saw a strange thing on the other side of the fence. He saw little watermelon sprouts by some rocks. He dug by the new plants and saw the old rinds with seeds sprouting. Immediately, he knew what had happened and the boy was caught.

When you've tried something and found it harmful, you cannot undo that experience. The damage is done, and you'll end up suffering the consequences of your actions. That is not a popular notion today in a world that is obsessed with finding a quick fix for every problem. Ours is a very shallow world, not prone to giving much thought to the link between problems and their underlying causes.

Ever heard of something called "jogging in a jug?" "Jogging in a Jug" is a concoction of four parts grape juice, four parts apple juice, and one part apple cider vinegar. Yum, yum! It's a folk remedy; a kind of "Drano" for your arteries. Supposedly, two ounces a day of this stuff and your insides will be as slick and clean as a whistle. Now, I don't know if it works. It's never been scientifically proven to do anything except cause you to make an awful face when you drink it. But wouldn't it be great if it did? Just the name sounds appealing: "Jogging in a Jug." Wouldn't it be great if you could gain all the benefits of jogging without actually having to exercise?! If you could lower your cholesterol and improve your health without having to strap on your Nikes and "just do it?" Or instead, you could "just drink it?" No getting up before dawn to drive to the gym; no hours of pain on the Stairmaster. Just a shot glass of vinegar and it's "please pass the Krispy Kreme doughnuts!"

Take another example. It used to be that if you ate junk food, you got fat. Now, we have Olestra, a fat substitute, so we can eat greasy potato chips and ice cream to our heart's content without raising our cholesterol. Over the years, we've developed a multitude of artificial sweeteners – cyclamates, saccharin, and aspartame – so we can drink all the sodas we want without rotting our teeth and expanding our middles. And if you do happen to eat something with actual fat or calories, you don't need to go to the gym to lose weight. All that sweating and huffing and puffing is so 80's. Now, you just make an appointment with your friendly local liposuctionist, and for a couple of thousand dollars, he or she will suck that fat right out.

In short, what we're constantly trying to do is repeal the law of sowing and reaping, sever the connection between action and consequence; not just with eating and drinking, but in every area of life. It's a universal human urge: people wanting to enjoy the benefits without paying the price.

Now, while you may be able to reverse the consequences of overeating, there's at least one area of life where the law of sowing and reaping always applies. And that's in our moral lives. Our character, our relationship with one another, these are ruled by the law of sowing and reaping. It's part of the moral fabric of the universe. This law can't be overturned by drinking vinegar. And so the way of wisdom is not to war against it, but to understand it, live by it and benefit from it. Ignoring the law of sowing and reaping only leads to sorrow and regret. What we need to do is respond to it in a way that's morally healthy.

Someone has said "As ye sow, so shall ye reap, unless of course you are an amateur gardener." This statement of jest reveals a great deal more of truth than we might like to admit.

This first law of the harvest sets us on our journey to a great harvest. But the key is to begin to sow today for tomorrow knowing it will make a difference in the lives coming behind us.

"The Only Preparation for Tomorrow is the Right Use of Today"

I love the story of Charlie Brown that clearly illustrates this point. Charlie Brown is seen at bat. "STRIKE THREE!" He has struck out again and slumps down on the players' bench. He says, "Rats! I'll never be a big league player. I just don't have it! All my life I've dreamed of playing in the big leagues, but I know I'll never make it."

Lucy turns to console him. "Charlie Brown, you're thinking too far ahead. What you need to do is set yourself more immediate goals." Charlie Brown looks up and questions, "Immediate goals?" Lucy responds, "Yes. Start with this next inning when you go out to pitch. See if you can walk out to the mound without falling down."

The first step toward a great harvest is the step you make today. Make it forward, well aimed and purposeful. The steps you take today become the well-worn path of tomorrow.

✳ ✳ ✳

Reflections

- If you reap what you so whether you want to or not, what seeds have you unknowingly planted in your life?

- What have been the consequences of planting unwanted seeds?

Begin to sow today for tomorrow knowing

it will make a difference in the lives coming

behind us.

2

We Reap the Same In Kind As We Sow

Everything reproduces after its kind. Just as no one can sow peas and produce watermelon, or breed donkeys and produce thoroughbred horses, so no one can sow evil and produce good. We cannot sow discord and produce unity. We cannot sow lies and produce truth.

The simplicity of this principle can be illustrated in two packs of seeds. I have a pack of yellow squash seeds and a pack of yellow sweet corn. Now according to the principle of this law, what do you suppose I will reap if I plant the corn? No doubt corn? And if I plant the squash, will I harvest squash? Of course!

It doesn't matter if I switch the seeds, to make myself think I am planting corn when I am planting squash. It is still squash! I can deny it and call it squash on the cob. But it is still squash! Why? Whatever a man sows, that he will also reap (Galatians 6:7b, NKJV).

Sow a thought, reap an act; sow an act, reap a habit. Sow a habit, reap a character; sow a character, reap a destiny.

One of the traits we have as human beings is the desire to live "independently" of our actions. As humans we want to believe that we can sow corn and get squash! In order for us to reap the same in kind as we sow, I have found that it is important to begin with the end in mind. What does that mean? No one plants a garden without first knowing what they want to harvest. As we sow corn seeds we begin to think about the end results, hot buttered corn on the cob!

We must begin to see the end of our sowing and consider if it is worth planting. This applies to the physical, emotional and spiritual realms of life. Each of us by our thoughts, attitudes, and actions is constantly planting for a future reaping. Time may pass before the crop ripens, but the harvest never fails. The true nature of the seed we have scattered will surely be revealed. But many of us have this uncanny ability to think, "This doesn't apply to me." If we sow to the flesh, we will reap the forces of corruption.

We cannot sow lies and produce truth.

We cannot sow discord and produce unity.

We must begin with the end in mind.

✳ ✳ ✳

Reflections

- What do you wish to harvest in your life? (Love, wealth, peace, good health, etc.)

- What are the specific seeds you need to plant to ensure you produce the harvest you desire?

Everything produces after its kind!

3

We Reap in a Different Season Thank We Sow

Many people do not think their actions/choices will catch up with them, but of course, it always does. Sooner or later our choices/actions return to haunt us. What we sow, we reap, but the thing that is so deceptive is that we reap in a different season. Because we do not see the immediate results, we often think we can or have gotten away with something, but we never do. We live in a self-oriented society that says "do your own thing," or "to thine own self be true." This is a society that has given over to instant gratification. We have instant everything: instant tea, instant oatmeal, quick rice, TV dinners, and microwave cooking. We can jump into an automobile and either whiz across town in minutes, across most states in a few hours, or board a plane and 12 hours later, land in Europe. We watch a TV program and see family conflicts or national conflicts resolved in one hour, or at the most in a mini-series, four hours, but in reality, these things often require months and even years to resolve or change. The younger generation today has the mentality of wanting and expecting to have all the material blessings and advantages their parents have. The difference is our parents often had to wait years to accumulate what they have. Young people are not willing to save, do without, and wait.   We want what we want when we want it which is usually right now, or preferably, yesterday. So, because we are accustomed to immediate gratification, we are too often unwilling to wait for the results of sowing—sowing what is good and waiting for the "crop" to ripen. No harvest comes the moment the seed is planted.

There are some things in life that are an acquired taste. Fried okra is one good example. I decided I'd like some fried okra for lunch today, so I bought some seeds this weekend. So I planted three okra seeds in this container of dirt. I carefully placed the seeds about an inch under the dirt, and have watered them. I am now waiting for them to grow so that I can pick, cut and fry the okra for lunch today. I can hardly wait! Only one thing troubles me. On the back of the okra seed package, it gives planting and harvesting instructions. It places a time difference between planting and harvesting, and it's called a season. It states, "Harvest in 50 days." Something tells me I won't be having fried okra today from these planted seeds. The third principle of the Laws of Harvest states, "We reap in a different season than we sow."

I. Sowing For Another Season

It is absurd to think we could plant okra seeds this morning and eat fried okra for lunch. But how often do we live our lives trying to sow and harvest in the same season? Let me confess my own failure to regard the laws of harvest. As a new educator, I had the opportunity to give a presentation at an event. After the event, I commented to a friend that I was a bit disappointed that more people had not come to listen to my talk. His reply to me was right on … "You cannot plant and harvest in the same season." You need to plant your seeds first and the harvest will come.

How right he was and how foolish I was to think I could sow and reap in the same season. The harvest never comes immediately after planting. The Bible tells us it comes in "due season." Ecclesiastes 3:1 (BSB)…"To everything there is a season, a time for every purpose under heaven."

This principle speaks to every area of our lives; married life, home life, children's life, dating life, work life, financial life, health life, church life, spiritual life; and last but not the least, eternal life. Because we too often operate on our emotions rather than on principles, we sow without regards to this particular principle.

II. Wanting What We Want When We Want It!

Living in an instant society we often lack the ability to wait. We are geared to things like "Jiffy Lube," drive-through banks to eateries, laser printers, and the internet. I read where a funeral home in California now has "drive-through viewing." We live life wanting quick and easy results. But it sows and reaps impatience with little or stunted growth.

Look how we bring this into our homes. How many are guilty of wishing their children would grow up? How many times have you said to your kids, "I wish you would grow up!"? There is a scene in the movie "Hook" where the all grown up Peter Pan says to his little boy, "Quit acting like a kid!" To which his son replies, "But I am a kid." We forget as adults we were once kids. Even now how foolish and childlike we are to plant the "rush & hurry up" seeds in our lives, and the lives of our children, with little regard to the results we will reap. We want what we want when we want it, and without regard to the laws of the harvest! We forget that the best things in life take time.

III. Because We Don't See Instant Results, We Believe There Will Be No Results.

To illustrate this disregard, let's use this piece of plastic called a credit card. The abuse of the plastic is easy to figure. We can purchase tens, hundreds and thousands of dollars in items without laying down one nickel. It tends to sow the idea we don't have to pay anything. I overheard the following conversation between a father and son at the department store while standing at the checkout counter: "Dad, do you have to pay for that?" The father's reply was, "Well, not today." Ah, but the law proves itself to be true. What we sow with the plastic we will reap a monthly statement with interest! Human nature is wired to instant gratification.

IV. Sowing Seeds of Goodness

Knowing what we know, what are we to do? I suggest we sow seeds of goodness, for in due season we shall reap if we do not lose heart. It's not enough to merely see the negative side of the ledger. We need to begin to fill the positive side of ledger today; to do the good works we are created for.

V. Sowing Seeds with Patience.

There's a word that is the essence of what this third principle is about. I like the following definitions of patience:

1. It's the ability to sit back and wait for an expected outcome without experiencing anxiety, tension, or frustration.

2. It's the ability let go of your need for immediate gratification and be willing to wait.

3. It's the trait that displays tolerance, compassion, understanding, and acceptance toward those who are slower than

you in developing maturity, emotional freedom, and coping abilities.

$$* * *$$

Reflections

- What areas do you need more patience in your life?

- Where in your life did you give up when it just wasn't time for yoru havest?

Sow a thought, reap an act

Sow an act, reap a habit.

Sow a habit, reap a character

Sow a character, reap a destiny.

4

We Reap More Than We Sow

No fact is more significant and sobering than this one. When a farmer sows his seeds, he expects the harvest to always be greater than the seed planted. If this were not the case, no farmer would ever plant a thing. If he only got back what germinated in the ground, he would be on the losing end and spend his life in utter futility. Reaping more than we sow is fundamental to the laws of the harvest and this is not just true for the agricultural

world; it is true for nearly every aspect of life. Of course,

there are some exceptions due to the fact that we live in a

world with natural and economic disasters. A farmer may

sow bountifully and have his crop destroyed by drought or

a tornado, or he may reap a good crop and not be able to

reap a reward from it because of economic factors in his

country.

What goes around, comes around. Every action has

a reaction. What goes up must come down. These are all

universal laws, laws that effect your life. There is also the

universal law of reaping and sowing. The laws of the

harvest seem so simple. Simple enough we may cast them

aside thinking nothing of them. But the complexity of each

law is that they powerfully produce a harvest of good

and/or bad in our lives. As I write, I am holding an apple in

my hand. This apple illustrates the point of this fourth law.

Having cut the apple in two pieces, we can count the

number of seeds contained in this apple. However, if we

were to keep the seeds for sowing season and wait for the harvest, we would be amazed how many apples we would reap from one seed. Someone has said, "You can count the number of seeds in an apple, but you can't count the number of apples in a seed."

I. The Measure of More

This law brings into our lives the simple truth of the "measure of more." It has been said, "The man who has more is the measure of all things."

We tend to believe and live by . . .

The more money you have, the better off you are.

The more power you have, the better chance you have of getting what you want.

The more prestige you have, the better chance you have of going somewhere.

However, we forget the law does not take into account what is better for us and the fact that it is left up to us in how and what we sow. This law only produces a harvest more than we have sown. It does not guarantee if the "more" is positive or negative because it is dependent

on what? What we have sown. But the law says that we

will reap MORE than what we sow.

II. A Biblical Example of More: Mark 4:1-8

In this parable, Jesus said that the seed that fell on

good ground increased (verse 8). A single grain grew to be

a plant that produced thirty, sixty, or a hundred more seeds.

Reaping more than we sow is fundamental to the laws of

the harvest. Every farmer lives by this principle. If his work

only returned exactly what he had planted in the ground,

his labor would be futile. He would never gain anything

extra with which to feed his family or sell for a profit.

Consider the potential of one kernel of corn: One kernel of

corn will produce one corn stalk. On the average, each stalk

will produce three ears. The average ear of corn has 250

kernels, so that a single kernel of corn will yield a 750%

increase.

The harvest is always greater than the seed planted

– whether we are speaking of agriculture or the things of

our lives. We invariably reap more than has been sown. This fact is both serious and sobering, and it applies equally to us humans. Whatever a person sows, whether good or bad, he will reap the benefits or the consequences in a significantly greater proportion. Of course, there are exceptions to this law because we live in a fallen world. A farmer may have his crops destroyed by drought, and we know that bad things can happen to good people. But even in these instances, if we look at the whole vision of a life, or all the seasons of harvest, we will find that as a general principle, we reap the same in kind as we have sown (Law Two) and we reap more than we have sown.

III. Negative Reaping of More

The farmer knows if he plants inferior/bad seed, he will get an inferior crop at harvest time, and sometimes "lots of it." I can hear the words of my mom, "B. Archie, you better be careful! You are going to get more than you bargained for." How right she was!

IV. Positive Reaping of More

Do We Really Reap What We Sow?

Looking into our ledger book we see this law, like the others has a positive column. In a typical apple orchard growers planted some of their trees 40 years ago. They continue to reap more than they planted in a very positive fashion. Do you think they would have planted those trees had they thought they would reap one apple for one tree planted? Of course not. The farmer who sows the seed has the expectation to reap a ratio of more than just "one to one." They intend to reap more than what was sown.

Let me remind you ...

Sow a thought and reap an act.
Sow an act and reap a habit.
Sow a habit and reap a character.
Sow a character and reap a destiny.

Moreover, sow a destiny and reap a legacy to be left for all those who come behind you. We sow more than we reap ... you can count on it.

✳ ✳ ✳

Reflections

- It's the little seeds that reap a big harvest. What are the little things you can do to ensure you receive the fruits of your labor?

5

We Reap in Proportion to What We Sow

C an a farmer plant one acre of crop and reap 100 acres worth? "If the farmer only cultivates one acre, he can only reap what one acre can produce." Let us examine the fifth law of the harvest to the aspect of our "doing." "We reap in proportion as we sow." This law identifies the quantity of the harvest to the proportion that has been sown. At first glance one might think this law is the same as the fourth law, "We reap more than you sow." But there is a difference. The last two laws deal with the fact we reap more than we sow. Both deal with quantity

and amount, but the previous law where the seed sown is

multiplied many folds, pertains to human responsibility. It

is synonymous with being bold, courageous, and

venturesome. The fourth law relates to life; the fifth law is

associated with "our part" in relations to how we sow.

I. Basis for this Principle

Principles govern our lives and are fundamental to

life. This law like all the others, is based upon principles.

Here's another way to look at it:

If you want to be rich … GIVE

If you want to be poor … GRASP

If you want abundance … SCATTER

If you want to be needy… HOARD

The law that "we reap in proportion to what we

sow," like all the laws of the harvest, operates both

negatively and positively. If we sow abundantly we will

reap abundantly in blessings and consequences. But if we

sow abundantly to the flesh, we will reap an abundant

harvest of the consequences of fleshly living—a life full of the weeds. David is a case in point: because David continued to sow to the flesh, his life snowballed. He went from coveting Bathsheba to lusting after another. He strayed abundantly and reaped abundant consequences. However, the primary motivation and emphasis of this principle and promise is toward the good. It is a spiritual law of life that is inherent to life, but one that is contrary to the nature of man.

II. Life's Uncertainties

Think of the following messages in Ecclesiastes 11: 1-6 NLT: "Give generously, for your gifts will return to you later. Divide your gifts among many, for you do not know what risks might lie ahead. When the clouds are heavy, the rains come down. When a tree falls, whether south or north, there it lies. If you wait for perfect conditions, you will never get anything done. Be sure to stay busy and plant a variety of crops, for you never know which will grow--perhaps they all will."

Do We Really Reap What We Sow?

Contrary to how man typically thinks, the verses above and the conditions they describe are designed to promote bountiful sowing, not the opposite which is stinginess. These verses warn about the dangers of being overly cautious which hinders generous sowing. The uncertainties of life are one of the things that keep most people from giving and ministering to others when they have the opportunity. They are afraid their giving will be their lack. Who knows what the future holds? If I give, I might not be able to meet the needs of my family. But these verses are given in a context that calls for generous giving knowing that our gifts will return to us later. The point here is don't try to second guess everything in life. We can't wait for conditions to be perfect. Nor can we wait for things to be free of all risks—absolutely free, absolutely safe. Instead of protecting ourselves, we have to take what appears to us as risks and live by faith.

6

We Reap the Full Harvest
Only if We Persevere

T his is a sobering principle of life. Experience in life teaches us that we reap the full harvest of the good only if we persevere, and bad things naturally comes to harvest on its own. It doesn't need our help. This is easily illustrated in gardening. It takes perseverance in cultivation to keep the weeds out and provide for conditions that promote healthy growth and fruitful plants, but weeds will naturally grow and take over a garden without doing a single thing. As mentioned above, anyone who has ever planted a garden knows that it cannot be planted and then forgotten. If it is, very little will come from the planting because of the many forces that work against a good harvest. A garden requires continuous labor and care in order to reap an abundant harvest. Reaping is related to the sowing, not only in the matter of the quality of the seed, but also in regard to the quantity sown. But the quantity sown is relative to the concept of endurance through the long haul. While diligence and perseverance in the present will produce proportionate abundance later, we are challenged to remember that laxity and fainting now produce proportionate poverty later. The need is perseverance in sowing. It's seldom easy, and sometimes we may not even see the fruits of our labor.

What goes around, comes around. Every action has a reaction. What goes up must come down. These are all universal laws, laws that effect our lives. Many of us have set aside a piece of acreage in our homes for use as a garden. In the summer it supports row after row of vegetation. Not everyone is involved in the gardening process, but the harvest always comes. A lot goes into the work before the vegetables are on your dinner table:

1. Cultivating the soil

2. Spreading of the fertilizer, better known as manure

3. Tilling the soil; going in a straight line!

4. Planting the seed.

5. Watering the soil

6. Culling the crops for proper growth. Pick out from others; remove rejected members or parts

7. Hoeing around the plants

The job of the gardener never stops. There is always something to do. When harvest time comes around, the work grows greater. A seasoned farmer will say, "It's time to get it up, work it up and store it up." Then comes the day of enjoying the produce from the land on your table. Fresh cut tomatoes, fried okra, and fresh corn on the cob. Are you getting hungry? Those of you who have helped with the process now have a greater appreciation for the perseverance of farmers who produce a good crop from the

garden. That brings us to the sixth law of the harvest which

is . . . "We reap the full harvest of the good only if we

persevere; the evil comes to harvest on its own." Let us

take a look into the realm of perseverance, that "keep on

keeping on" aspect in life.

I. Persevering In Working

Albert Bean has said, "To know and not do is not

yet to know." Probably all of us could readily say

concerning the hard, persevering work prior to the harvest,

"I know that!" Those who have gardens know that you

cannot plant and forget. Very little will come from such

gardening techniques. A garden requires a lot of labor if

you are going to reap an abundant harvest. Someone has

said, "The problem of the average person today is not a

lack of knowledge, but the application of truths he already

knows." The knowledge I am referring to here is not simply

the "know how" of which you will most surely respond,

"Oh, I know that." But true knowledge is the "applying" of

what we know and doing it in all aspects of our lives. Thus we can say, "I do that because I know." So the question is have we become the fool who hates knowledge and who casually rejects the knowledge? Without true knowledge leading us to do, how can we persevere in hard times?

II. Persevering In Weeds

A gardener has to plant seeds for the harvest, but he doesn't have to plant weeds. They come about on their own. "... The evil comes to harvest on its own." Weeds are defined as "a plant considered undesirable, worthless unattractive, or troublesome, useless and detrimental, especially one growing where it is not wanted." One of the most difficult parts of gardening is having to keep up with the weeds. Why? It is a never-ending job. No sooner than you finish weeding a row of crops, the weeds spring up at the beginning of the row! In the midst of weeds we must:

i. Persevere in the weeding.

We must eradicate from our lives the things that hinder the harvest. Someone has said, "Somehow we have the feeling that if we do things right, there should be no

problems." In other words, we think if we have properly

done all the cultivation, planting, and watering there should

be no weeds. Ah, but the weeds come on their own. So why

persevere? We need to continue the work in our lives even

in the midst of the weeds.

ii. Persevere in the goal.

Before Moses was ready to lead the children of

Israel, he needed the education of being raised in Egypt and

leading sheep for his father-n-law. Before David was ready

to be king over Israel he needed to trust and wait on God's

timing. While on the run from Saul, David learned to know

the people he would be king over. Now if you are not an

experienced farmer and you help in the garden, you will

probably find yourself crying the blues: "This is too hard.

When are we going to be done? Why are the weeds coming

back?" But you'll never hear the farmer complain. Just as

in gardening, in life too, we should persevere and not give

up and let the weeds have the garden. Persevere and let the

weeds cause you to enjoy the harvest that much more!

iii. Persevering In Waiting

Have you discovered that there are times we can do nothing but wait? It's the third law of the harvest, "We reap in a different season than we sow." Yes, we are encouraged to work and to weed. But we must also learn to wait. See how the farmer waits for the precious fruit of the earth, waiting patiently for it until it receives the early and latter rain? In our inability to wait, we could easily pass the buck off onto our "fast and instantaneous" society. However, it comes down to the fact we lack maturity in a true knowledge of life; thus we become impatient in many things we do. Hudson Taylor, founder of the China Inland Mission once said, "I used to ask God if He would come and help me. Then I asked God if I might come and help Him. Then I ended by asking God to do His work through me."

iv. Persevering In Hope

Perseverance is not just adjusting to the things that are around us or come upon us. Perseverance looks beyond the now to see and know the harvest is coming! A key to perseverance is "hope." I came across a very funny "hope" story which I would like to share: While hunting, Larry and Elmer got lost in the woods. Trying to reassure his friend, Larry said, "Don't worry. All we have to do is shoot into the air three times, stay where we are, and someone will find us." They shot in the air three times, but no one came. After a while, they tried again. Still no response. When they decided to try once more, Elmer said, "I hope it works this time. We're down to our last three arrows."

Larry and Elmer put their hope in the advice of others, even though they didn't understand that the advice didn't apply to shooting arrows. People in difficult circumstances often rely on advice of friends, neighbors, and experts. Just like Larry and Elmer, they will listen to others, placing their hope in the wisdom and experience of those they trust. But sometimes, they do fail us.

∗ ∗ ∗

Reflections

- You cannot neglect what you plant. What seeds in your life need more of your time and attention?

If you want to be rich ... GIVE
If you want to be poor ... GRASP
If you want abundance ... SCATTER
If you want to be needy... HOARD

7

We Can't Do Anything About Last Year's Harvest, But We Can About This Year's.

L ife is full of consequences, both good and bad. Life is full of important choices because every choice has a consequence of some kind and to some degree. Actually, the most important choices are often the ones that seem small by comparison, but these are the ones which may either protect us or expose us to choices that have tremendous repercussions. But how do we handle it when last year's harvest is not so good, when we have fumbled the ball or failed? The tendency is to let our failure keep us from positive sowing today. What we must understand and act on is this final law of the harvest—We cannot do anything about last year's harvest, but we can about this year's. This law translates into at least four important concepts that we need to understand and apply if we are going to be able to act on this law:

(1) We cannot do anything about last year's harvest.

(2) We must learn to live with the consequences of our failures.

(3) We must commit ourselves to this year's harvest.

(4) We must not judge our harvest by the standards of the world and its ideas of success.

WE CANNOT DO ANYTHING ABOUT LAST YEAR'S HARVEST: Whatever we did last year, last month, last week, even yesterday is over and passed. There are no time machines to take us back so we can change what we did yesterday. Nothing we do today can in any way change the record of what was sown and what was or will be reaped as a consequence. The problem with all too many people is that they are not forgetting the past and reaching on to what is before.

WE MUST LEARN TO LIVE WITH THE CONSEQUENCES OF OUR FAILURES: When people believe they are failures or that their failures forever ruin their chances for success and marks them for life, it neutralizes them and wipes out their ability to use their life to the fullest.

WE MUST COMMIT OURSELVES TO THIS YEAR'S HARVEST: We must press on in our lives by sowing for the future. Whether we did or did not produce effectively in last year's harvest, we must neither sit around in self-pity or guilt, nor sit on our laurels. We must press on toward the goal.

WE MUST NOT JUDGE OUR HARVEST BY THE STANDARDS OF THE WORLD: It is hard to face failure because it is so ugly and devastating, but our failures can become ladder to success. We have a hard time admitting that the road to victory is often filled with speed bumps, pot holes, accidents, and detours. In his book, Failure, The Back Door to Success, Erwin Lutzer writes, "We judge ourselves and others by a false standard. If we judge ourselves on the basis of possessions, acceptance, names and number, then many of us would be failures. We use the wrong yardstick to measure success; by things like who they know, by comparing results, personal gifts and abilities, clothes, cars, houses, popularity, and fame."

The "War Cry" magazine reminds us of an important principle. "A loose wire gives out no musical note; but fasten the ends, and the piano, the harp, or violin is born. Free steam drives no machine but hamper and confine it with piston and turbine and you have the great world of machinery made possible. The unhampered river drives no dynamos, but dam it up and we get power sufficient to light a great city. So, our lives must be disciplined if we are to be of any real service in this world."

Again, while we should never want to fail, we all do and we need to learn to use our failures as stepping stones to growth and development.

Here's a poem that goes with the theme of what we've been studying:

"If Turnip Seed Grow Turnips"

If turnip seeds grow turnips, And greens grow spinach greens;

If carrot seeds grow carrots, And bean seeds bring up beans;

If lettuce seeds grow lettuce, And brussel seeds grow sprouts;

If pea seeds always bring up peas – Then what goes in comes out!

So kind words bring up kindness, And bad words will grow sadness;

Forgiving words will grow forgiveness, Glad words will grow gladness!

So watch the little seeds you plant, In all you say and do;

For what you sow is what you reap! Be proud of what you

grew!

1. Let Us Go On

Have you ever thought about "time travel?"

Wouldn't it be great if movies like "Time Machine" and

"Back to the Future" could be a reality? Think of all we

could go back and change or do differently. Why we could

go all the way back to the Garden of Eden and correct that

original sin and poof ... everything is okay. Yes, those are

great thoughts, but you and I know that whatever we did

yesterday, last week, last month and even last year is over

and it is called the "past." We cannot do anything about

last year's harvest. Furthermore, each of these laws

concentrates on the today. Of course, they remind us of

yesterday and tomorrow, but they speak to us of what we

are to sow today. What is the lesson from this law? If last

year we failed to produce a worthy crop, we don't need to

view ourselves as failures and be upset over the past. And if we produced a good crop last year, we do not need to rest, thinking this year's crop will come up its own. This seventh law teaches us to "go on." Since we cannot do anything about the past, we must move on.

2. How do we go on?

i). You must "deal with your mistakes."

A difficult lesson we all must learn is that we are absolutely, totally and completely unable to pay the price for our own mistakes. In society we have an idea of justice that works on a limited basis. For example, if you rob a bank you pay your "debt to society" by serving time in prison. Of course, if you ask anyone who has been to prison they will tell you that even after they served their time, the debt wasn't really paid in full. The stigma of having been in jail follows them for the rest of their life. It makes it difficult to get a job, to get bonded, to vote, to be in a serious relationship--you may serve your debt to society, but society doesn't forget the debt. There's an old Humphrey Bogart movie called "Invisible Stripes" about an ex-con trying to make it on the outside, but everything

seems to be stacked against him. He's wearing invisible

stripes, and no matter what he does, they'll never disappear.

We wear stripes, too. No matter how we try, we cannot pay

for our own mistakes. You can't "unrob" a bank. You can't

"unsay" hateful words. Once milk has been spilled, you

can't "unspill" it. There's nothing we can do to pay for our

own mistakes.

ii). You must "let go of the past."

Too many people live in the past. They fail to forget

and move on to what life has for them today with

tomorrow. One of the reasons we cannot move forward is

that too many of us drop the ball all too often. We live in

our past day after day. We remind ourselves how terrible

we are and what awful things we have done. As a result,

just like Humphrey Bogart, we go through life with

invisible stripes--and we allow them to hold us back. Don't

be a prisoner to the past. Let go of it.

iii). You must "focus on what you can do for your

future."

When you examine the life of Christ and see how he related to people, something quickly becomes obvious: Jesus cares more about your future than He does about your past. A great example is Zacchaeus was a Jew, but he was despised by other Jews. He built a personal fortune by extorting exorbitant taxes from his own countrymen and skimming some off the top for himself. When he heard that Jesus was coming to town, he desperately wanted to see him, but he was short in height and couldn't see over the crowd. So he climbed to the top of a Sycamore tree and waited for Jesus to pass by. When Jesus reached the spot where Zacchaeus was, He said, "Zacchaeus, come down. I must stay at your house today." People criticized Jesus for eating with a sinner, but Jesus wasn't concerned with Zacchaeus ' past, he was concerned with his future. That day Zacchaeus the sinner became Zacchaeus the saint. He turned his back on the past and began to concentrate on his future as a follower of Christ. In his conviction, he said he'd give back twice of what he had taken from the people.

In 1986, Bob Brenley was playing third base for the San Francisco Giants. In the fourth inning of a game against the Atlanta Braves, Brenley made an error on a routine ground ball. Four batters later, he kicked away another grounder. And then while he was scrambling after the ball, he threw wildly past home plate trying to get the runner out. Instantly, two errors on the same play! A few minutes later, he muffed yet another play to become the first player in the twentieth century to make four errors in one inning. Now, those of us who have made very public errors in one situation or another can easily imagine how he felt during that long walk off the field at the end of that inning. But in the bottom of the fifth, Brenley hit a home run! Then in the seventh, he hit a bases-loaded single, driving in two runs and tying the game. Afterwards in the bottom of the ninth, Brenley came up to bat again, with two outs. He ran the count to three and two and then hit a massive home run into the left field seats to win the game for the Giants! Brenley's score card for that day came to three hits, five at bats, two home runs, four errors, four runs allowed, and four runs driven in, including the game-winning run.

Certainly life is a lot like that--a mixture of hits and errors. And thankfully, there is grace in that. Your life may seem like a desert, but know that it can become an oasis. You can turn the page around and write something new in your life; it is your job to let go of the past and concentrate on what you can do in your life today and tomorrow. Regardless of what brought you to where you are today, you can do something to change your story. Now, let go of the past, and concentrate on living today.

✳ ✳ ✳

Reflections

- A farmer has no choice but to keep planting even after a year of a poor harvest. Where do you feel stuck in your life? What has you focused on what didn't happen, as opposed to hwat can happen for your future?

We must not judge our harvest by the standards of the world.

Final
Thoughts

What Are You Sowing and What Do You Hope to Reap?

E As I finish this chapter, I write from the inside of a train, returning from a professional conference where I had been speaking all week long. I am tired, exhausted and weary. Suddenly, the train took a small bend and in front of me were fields of thousands upon thousands of bright red poppies, gently swaying in the wind. Fields of poppies, obviously growing wild, spread over miles of the countryside. I was

mesmerized by the beauty and found myself wondering

how long it had taken for these beautiful flowers to be

planted over the years so that there would be so many

everywhere. I began to imagine nature's invisible hand

intentionally spreading seed generously over the many

fields, so that in a country where there had been and still is

so much division, war and darkness for so many

generations, that there would still be a picture of nature's

beauty and life to comfort those who would see it. As an

educator, this has become to me a sort of picture of my

place in the world; the sower of seeds into the lives of the

students I teach.

Those who sow with tears will reap with joy.

We are all sowers of seeds when we invest in the

lives of friends, family and our children. As I look out the

window at the fields of wild poppies, it gives me a sense of

what we must do to bring in the harvest; we must sow the

seeds of patience, perseverance, love, joy, seed by seed, so that our harvest will be plentiful. We must sow seeds daily, weekly; for our whole lives, that there will be remnants of beauty, peace, redemption, everywhere we go, every day that we live. If we sow peace and not anger in our home, there will be a legacy of peace. It is a choice we make, every day, every hour, as to what we are sowing and what we will reap. The seeds I sow are in relationship to people in my life every day. I must make a decision in my heart to sow a seed of peace where there is strife--to choose to be a peace-maker and to sow love and redemption. I must sow seeds of encouragement and faith through my words and through my writings to bring others to the point of peace in their own lives. Seed by seed, choice by choice, we all have the ability to bring about a great harvest in our lives. But in order for a farmer to have a harvest, he must plan on what he will sow, he must plan the seeds he will plant---it doesn't happen by chance. So, I must choose what crop I will sow, how I will sow it, and choose to sow it in each situation and in each relationship that comes my way. Peace, love, joy,

and success do not just happen by chance. There had to be

an intentional plan.

I know there are those who will criticize my

Pollyanna approach to life. By no means am I espousing

that I only see and report the positive things in life or that I

put forth only those things which I think are perfect. I hope

that I never give the impression that I am perfect, or that

our children, our families or anything else is perfect. I

would hate to impose guilt on anyone, by creating false

standards through the stories I have shared that someone

else feels they can't immolate. I hope instead to always

point us all to some basic truths in life. As a matter of fact,

I have only made it this far because I so depend on God's

grace and when I feel inadequate or like a failure, which I

think we all do from time to time, there is a place I have

trained myself to go and that is where Jesus is. I tell Him

how I am feeling and then by faith, I acknowledge how

grateful I am that He has made me adequate in Himself, by His strength, through His love and for His glory. Here is where I seek to rest. Remaining, simmering and swimming in the sea of guilt is destructive and heart-killing. I have discovered that no matter how hard I try I often fall short of my own expectations---let alone the expectations of others. If this is true of me that I fail, even when trying, then I must understand that even the best and most mature person I know, will also fail themselves and me too. So, my choice in sharing my writings and my life, is to give us all a picture of ideals for which we can strive, in the context of the messy world in which we live. I want to be the sower of a picture of beauty, a field of hope, and pattern of unconditional love in the midst of fields of life where there are weeds, rocks and untilled ground.

I have had a history of people very close to me who live in anger and criticism. This sowing of strife has left a string of broken relationships, deep hurt, and alienation.

Do We Really Reap What We Sow?

Sometimes I am afraid to be around these people because

no matter how hard I try or what I say or do, I know that

eventually I will do something to arouse their criticism

again. (I am choosing not to name these people as they are

very close to me and I don't want to intentionally hurt

them.) I used to think that if I just tried hard enough or did

enough, eventually I would receive the acceptance I was

looking for. But it took many years, to realize that their

anger and criticism had nothing to do with me and no

matter how hard I tried, I would never be acceptable to

them, because the problem was in their own dark and

hurting heart. But in order to have in my heart a harvest of

peace, and not bitterness or anger; and a harvest of love and

not hate and retaliation, I had to seek to plant seeds of love,

joy and faithfulness, to ensure my heart would truly bear a

harvest worth celebrating. This required that I pondered

what it meant to be a good example, to love others

especially when that love is not returned, to understand that

love covers a multitude of flaws, to learn that Jesus

Himself, when He was being crucified, "did not revile in return, but kept trusting Himself to God who judges righteously." (1Peter 2:23) He has become my model--that I would choose not to revile those who were angry or negative, but that I, like Jesus, would keep trusting myself to God---to place my issues in His file cabinets and to let Him deal with my difficulties, and then to close the drawer once these issues were safe in His hands.

Instead of hoping that those near me would love me in such a way as to make me feel good about myself, I just kept reading the Word everyday----seeking to know my God better, pondering the stories of Jesus, thinking about His communication to me through how He lived and what He said. Now, as I am getting older, I find His love to be deeply satisfying. After literally thousands of hours in His presence over the years, I have been influenced by being in the company of someone so compassionate, loving and strong. I have made peace with Him and appreciate Him. In doing so, I learned that I could give that peace more easily to others, because I didn't have as many expectations of them and I wasn't as dependent on how they responded to me, in order to feel good about myself. However, I see a lot of people wasting time, effort and energy in being critical of others close to themselves. There is a lot of anger, disappointment, jealousy, hate and bitterness floating around in the lives of people, which color their view of life, suck the energy out of them. It is so easy to be critical of a family member, wallow in unmet expectations, or friends who have forsaken us. Or in a child who has gone astray or is just immature or has a personality flaw that drives us crazy, or a parent who has abused or rejected us for our values.

It starts with a choice

We all have to decide ahead of time to imagine what it looks like to be at peace and have joy at each moment in our lives; to choose to sow righteousness into our relationships. I believe that if many of us chose to sow this way each day, on all of the fields of our lives, there would be such a great crop of righteousness, beauty and love. Even in times where so much darkness exists, many hearts would be open because of the overwhelming crop of righteousness present before their eyes. But it all begins with a choice in our heart and a plan to sow today, this day, in these fields where we find ourselves. Whoever and whatever it is that brings emotional disappointment can keep us from experiencing love in our lives, if we never make it to the point of forgiveness and acceptance of the person and circumstances. I know how deeply it can hurt to be rejected, ignored or treated unjustly. I have shed many tears over many years. Yet, I can honestly say, that it has been these difficulties that have brought me to a place of

freedom and joy. I have desperately needed the grace of

God and in so seeking it, I have found it to be deeper than I

could ever imagined. He has shown me how deep His love

is for me and how much He wants me to give as deeply to

those in my life, who like me, don't deserve it, but need it

all the same.

About the Author

Dr. Nguh is a Professor in the Graduate Nursing program with Walden University where he has a double appointment in the Master of Nursing and PhD in the Public Health program. Additionally, he serves as chair of dissertation committee for PhD in Public Health program. Prior to joining Walden University, Dr. Nguh was the Chair of Graduate Nursing program at Kaplan University where he oversaw the MSN program and developed the curriculum for the DNP program. Prior to that he was the

Do We Really Reap What We Sow?
Director of Nursing at the University of the District of

Columbia, Washington D.C.

Dr. Nguh holds a PhD in Public Health from

Walden University, a Master of Science in Nursing from

the University of Dundee in the UK, a Master of Science in

Healthcare Administration from Strayer University and a

Bachelor of Science in Nursing from Walden University.

Dr. Nguh holds numerous fellowships including the

American College of Healthcare Executive, the National

Academies of Practice, and certification as Nurse

Executive, Advanced from the American Nurses

Credentialing Center. Dr. Nguh is a five-time national

award winner for his work in community service and

volunteerism. In 2015, he was honored by the National

League of Nursing with the Lillian Wald Humanitarian

Award, and the Outstanding Mentor Award from the

Maryland Nurses Association (2015) and the Nurse of the

Year Award from Nurse.com (2012). Dr. Nguh sits on

several healthcare boards including the regional chapter of

Nurse.com, the Maryland Nurses Association, and the American College of Healthcare Executives (National Capital Chapter).